Rock *Ballads*

THE SOFT SIDE OF HARD ROCK

Produced by
Alfred Music Publishing Co., Inc.
P.O. Box 10003
Van Nuys, CA 91410-0003
alfred.com

Printed in USA.

ISBN-10: 0-7390-9375-4
ISBN-13: 978-0-7390-9375-7

Alfred Cares. Contents printed on 100% recycled paper.

Artist Index

Contents

BREATHE

Words by
ROGER WATERS

Music by
ROGER WATERS, DAVID GILMOUR
and RICK WRIGHT

Breathe - 8 - 1

Verse 1:

8

Breathe - 8 - 5

Verse 2:

Run,__ rab - bit, run!__

gradual gliss.

*past fingerboard

Dig that hole,___ for - get__ the sun.___

10

When,___ at last,___ the work___ is   done,___

gradual gliss.

even gliss.

don't_ sit down,___ it's time_ to dig___ an-oth - er one.   For

Chorus:

long you live__ and high__ you fly,_____ but on - ly if___ you ride__ the tide._____ And

bal - anced on__ the big - gest wave, race to - wards__ an ear - ly grave.

BROKEN

(featuring Amy Lee)

Words and Music by
SHAUN WELGEMOED
and DALE STEWART

Slowly ♩ = 62

Intro:

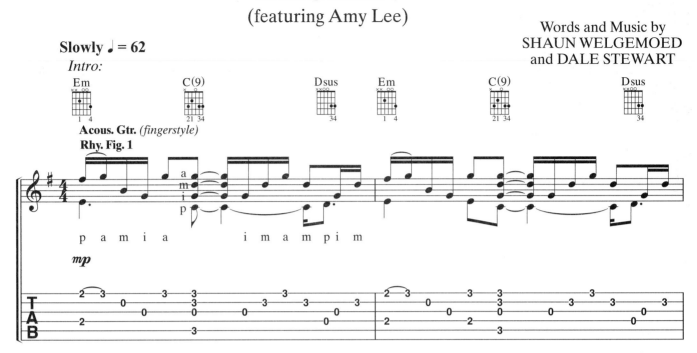

Verse:

1. I want-ed you to know___ that I love the way you laugh.___
2. The worst is o - ver now___ and we can breathe a - gain.___

Broken - 6 - 1

I wan - na hold you high and steal your_ pain_____ a - way.
I wan - na hold you high, you steal my_ pain_____ a - way.

I keep your pho - to - graph,_ I know it serves me well._
There's so much left to learn_ and no one left me to fight._

I wan - na hold you high and steal your_ pain._____ 'Cause I'm
I wan - na hold you high and steal your_ pain._____ 'Cause I'm

Cont. in slashes

Chorus:

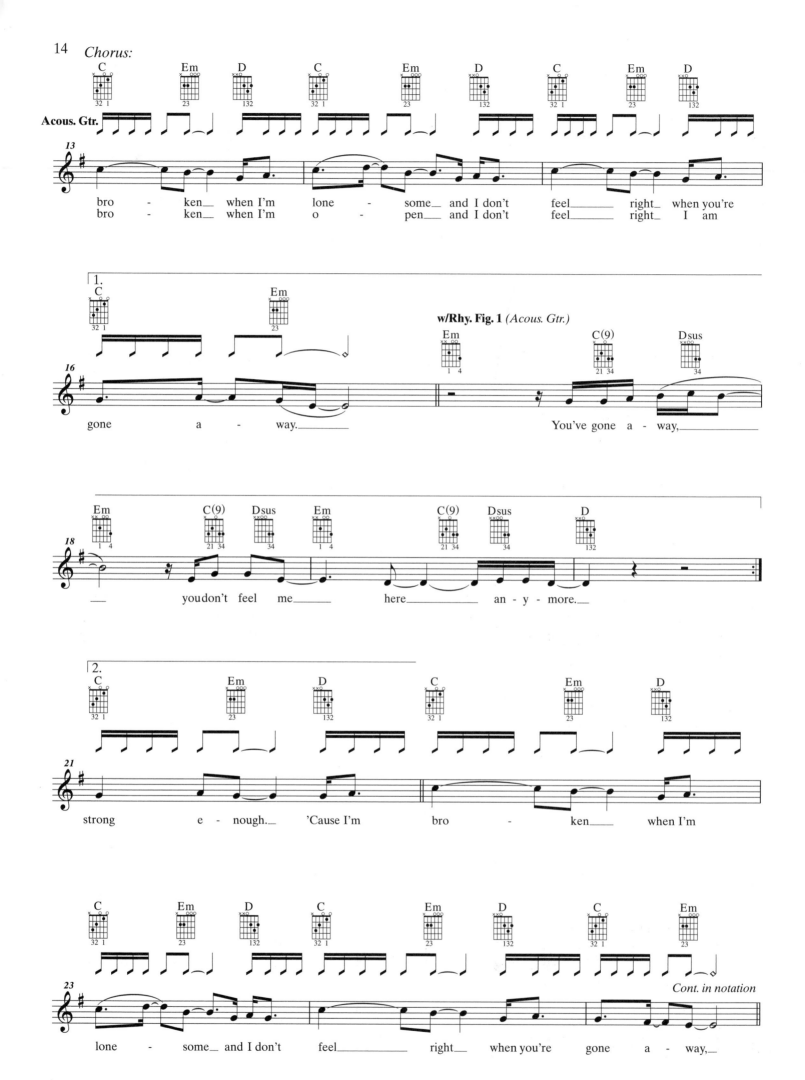

Guitar Solo:

'Cause I'm

16

'Cause I'm

Chorus:

bro - ken___ when I'm lone - some___ and I don't

feel___ right___ when you're gone a - way.___

Outro:

You're gone a - way,___ you don't feel me___

___ here___ an - y - more.___

EUROPA (EARTH'S CRY HEAVEN'S SMILE)

Music by
CARLOS SANTANA and TOM COSTER

Europa (Earth's Cry Heaven's Smile) - 7 - 1

FOUNTAIN OF SORROW

Words and Music by
JACKSON BROWNE

To match record key, Capo I

Moderately ♩ = 126
Intro:

Verse 1:

Look-ing through_ some pho-to-graphs_ I found in-side a draw-er,_ I was

tak-en by__ a pho-to-graph_ of you._____ There were

one or two__ I know that I___ would have liked__ a lit-tle__ more,_____ but they

Fountain of Sorrow - 5 - 1

Outro:

Repeat and fade

Verse 3:
Now for you and me it may not be that hard to reach our dreams,
But that magic feeling never seems to last.
And while the future's there for anyone to change,
Still you know it seems
It would be easier sometimes to change the past.
(To Pre-chorus 3:)

Pre-chorus 3:
I'm just one or two years and a couple of changes behind you.
In my lessons at love's pain and heartache school;
Where if you feel too free and you need something to remind you,
There's this loneliness springing up from your life
Like a fountain from a pool.
(To Chorus:)

FAITHFULLY

Words and Music by
JONATHAN CAIN

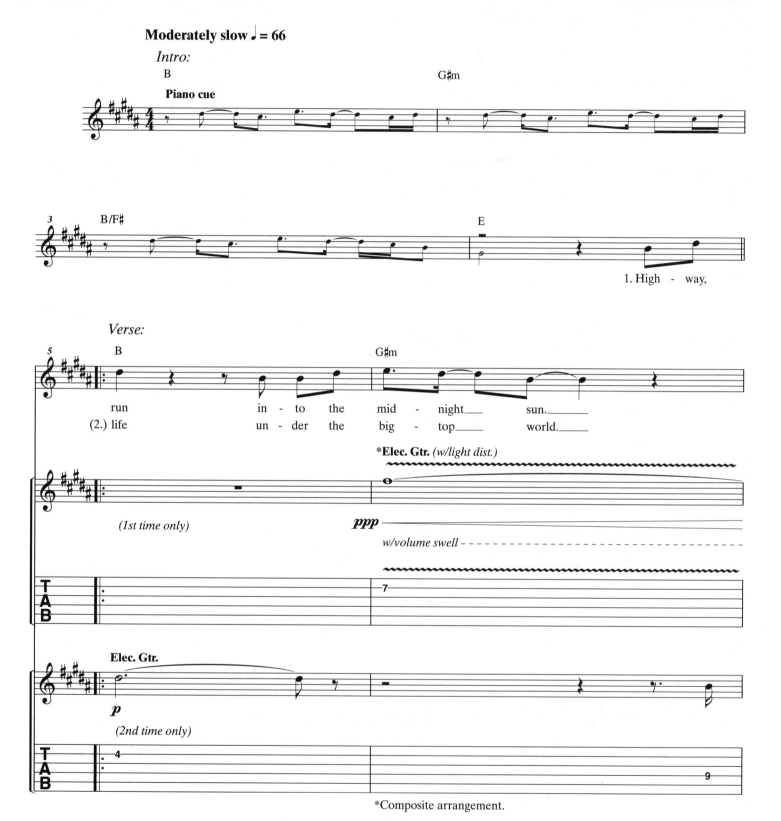

*Composite arrangement.

Faithfully - 6 - 1

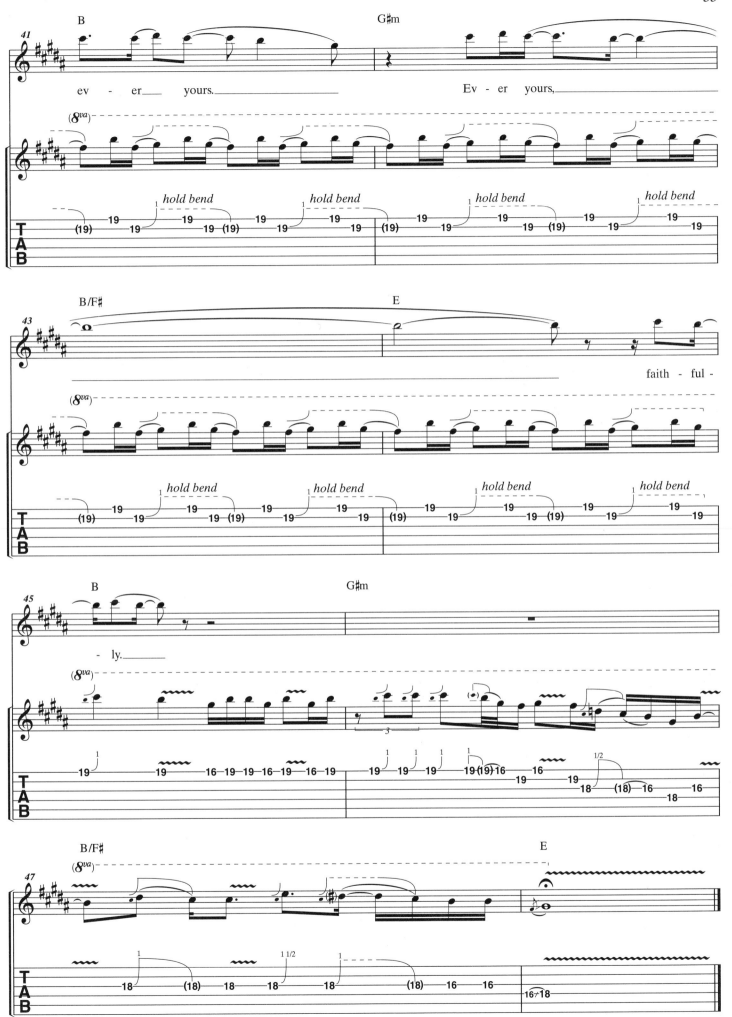

THE GAME OF LOVE

(featuring Michelle Branch)

Words and Music by
GREGG ALEXANDER and RICK NOWELLS

*Composite arrangement.

The Game of Love - 11 - 1

The Game of Love - 11 - 2

46

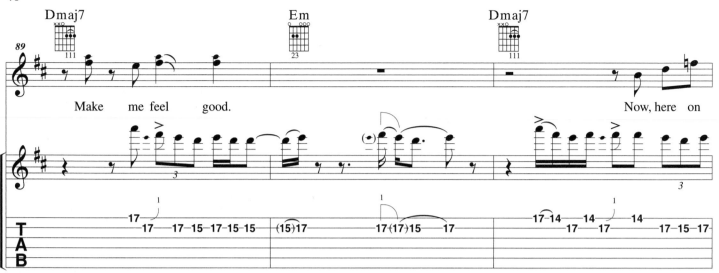

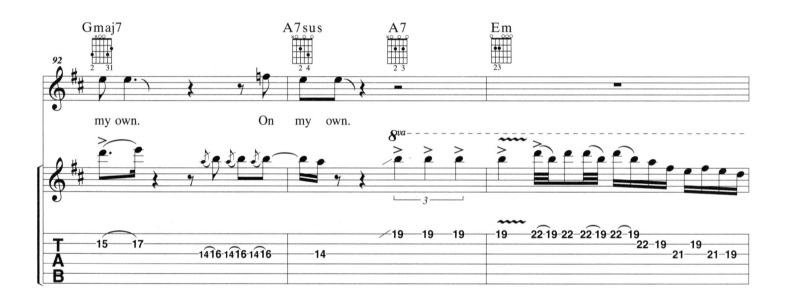

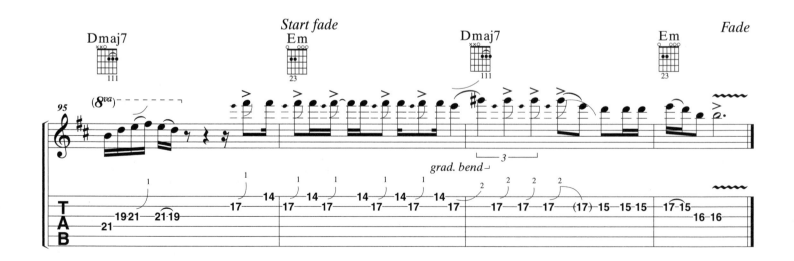

HIGHER

Gtr. tuned in Drop D:
⑥ = D ③ = G
⑤ = A ② = B
④ = D ① = E

Words and Music by
MARK TREMONTI and SCOTT STAPP

Slow rock ♩ = 80

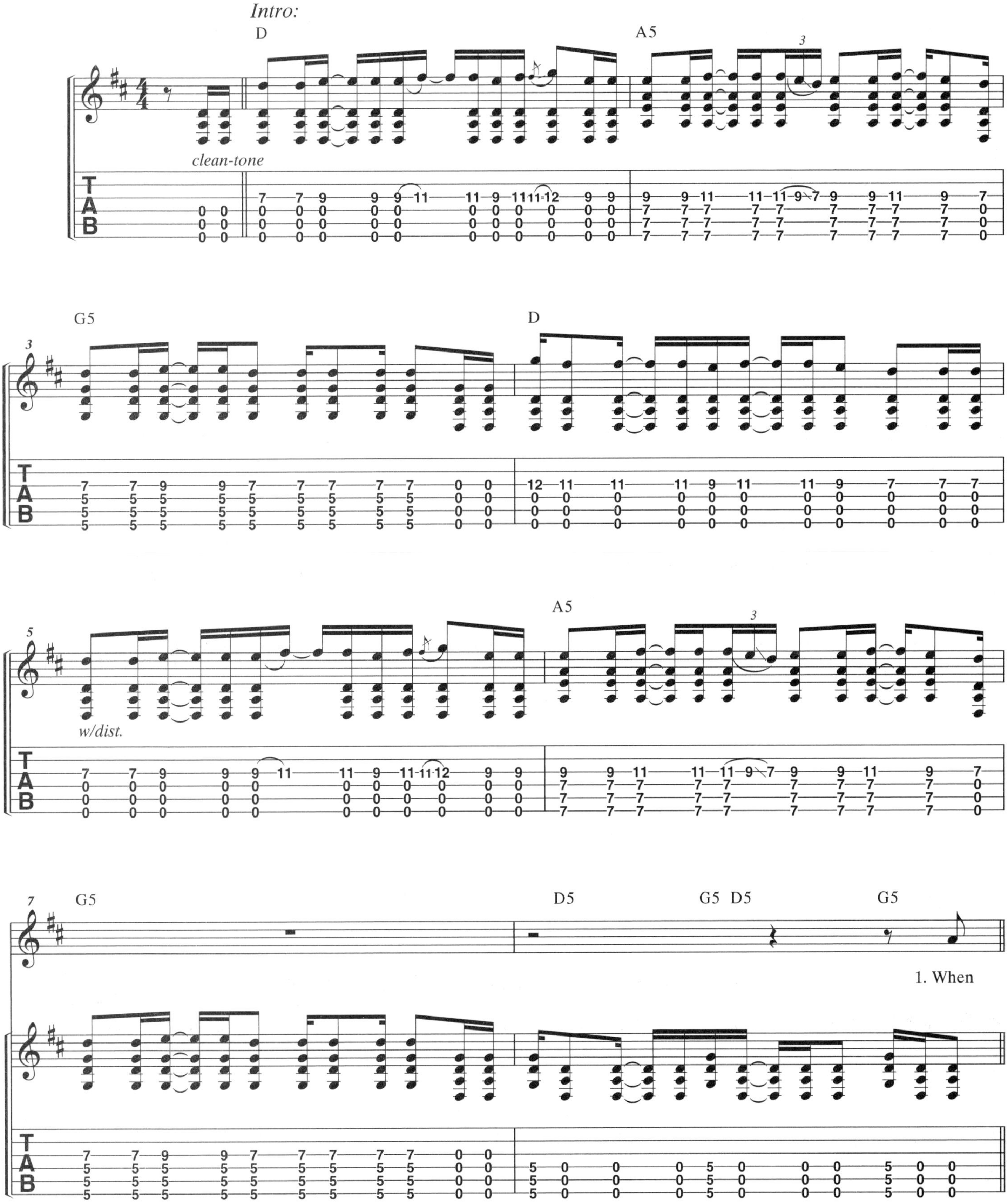

Intro:

clean-tone

w/dist.

1. When

Higher - 7 - 1

Chorus:

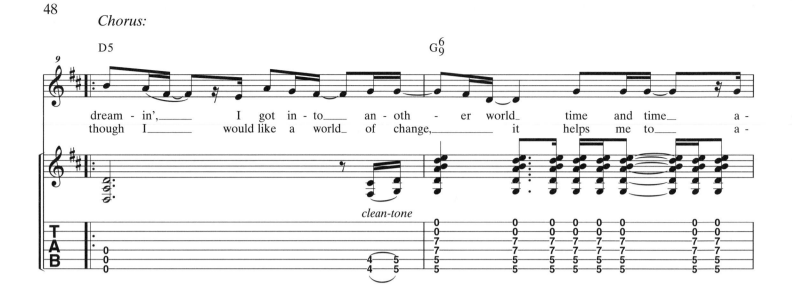

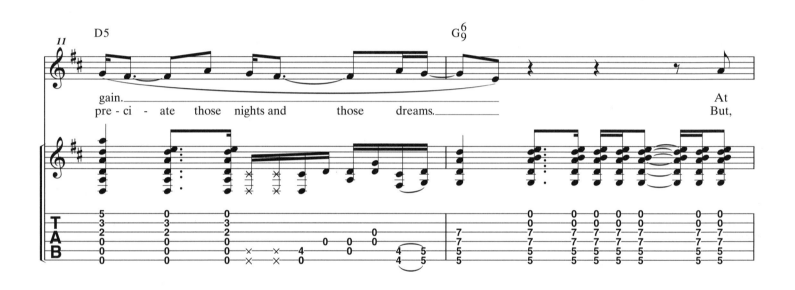

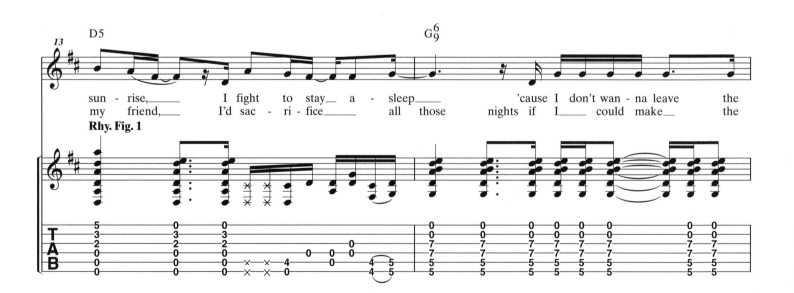

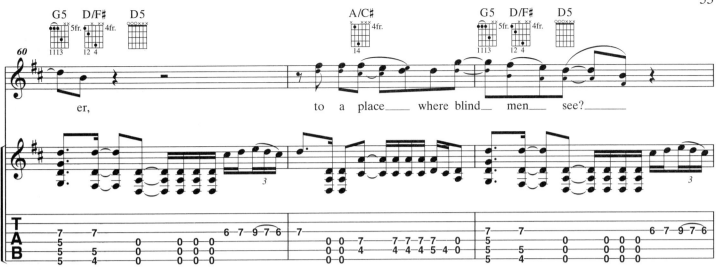

er, to a place____ where blind____ men____ see?

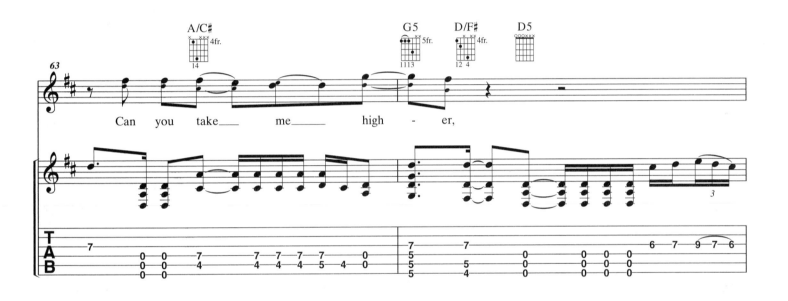

Can you take____ me____ high - er,

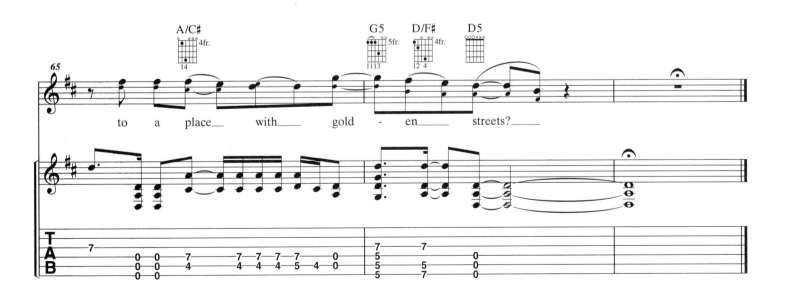

to a place____ with____ gold - en____ streets?____

HANDY MAN

Words and Music by
OTIS BLACKWELL and JIMMY JONES

*Capo 2nd fret to match pitch of recording.

Handy Man - 4 - 1

I whis - per sweet things; you tell all your friends.___

𝄋 Pre-chorus:

Gtrs. resume primary rhythm

They'll come run - nin' to me._____ Here is the main thing that

I want to say:____ I'm bus - y twen - ty - four___ hours___ a day.____ I

To Coda ⊕ **w/Rhy. Fig 1** *(Acous. Gtr.) simile*

fix bro - ken hearts. { I know,___ but I tru - ly can.___ | Ba - by, I'm your___ hand - y man.___

Chorus:

Acous. Gtr. resume secondary rhythm

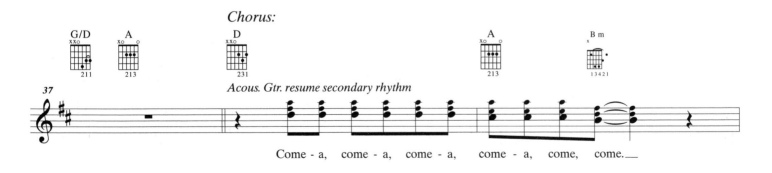

Come - a, come - a, come - a, come - a, come, come.___

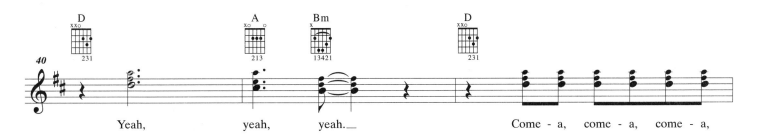

Yeah, yeah, yeah.— Come - a, come - a, come - a,

D.S. % al Coda

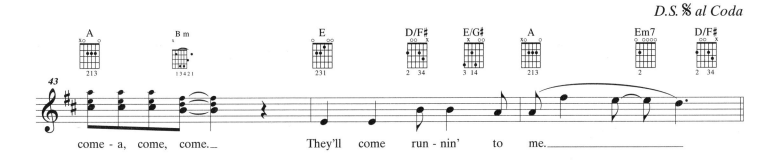

come - a, come, come.— They'll come run - nin' to me.—

w/Rhy. Fig. 1 *(Acous. Gtr.) simile*   *Chorus:*

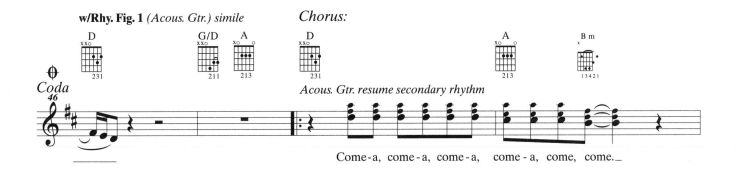

Coda

Acous. Gtr. resume secondary rhythm

Come-a, come-a, come-a, come - a, come, come.—

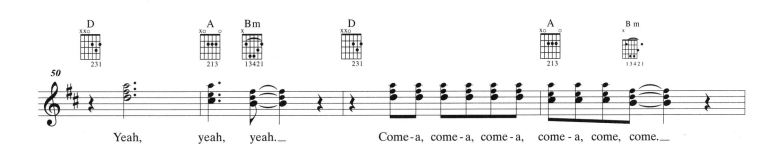

Yeah, yeah, yeah.— Come-a, come-a, come-a, come - a, come, come.—

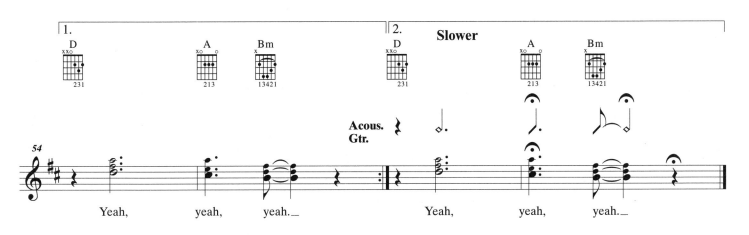

1. **2.** **Slower**

Acous. Gtr.

Yeah, yeah, yeah.— Yeah, yeah, yeah.—

Handy Man - 4 - 4

IF YOU LEAVE ME NOW

*To match record key, Capo II

Words and Music by
PETER CETERA

Moderately slow ♩ = 102

Intro:

*Recording sounds a whole step higher than written.

Verse 1:

leave__ me now,__ you'll take a - way__ the big - gest part__ of me.__ Ooh,_____

_____ no,__ ba - by, please_____ don't go._____ And if you

If You Leave Me Now - 4 - 1

leave__ me now,__ you'll take a - way__ the ver - y heart__ of me.__

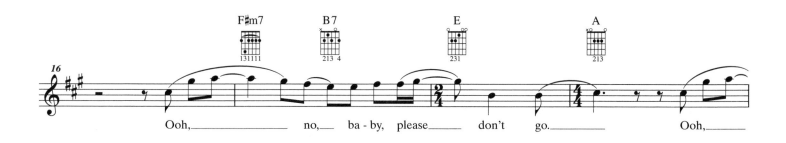

Ooh,__ no,__ ba - by, please__ don't go._____ Ooh,_____

_____ girl,__ I just want you to stay._____

℅ Bridge:

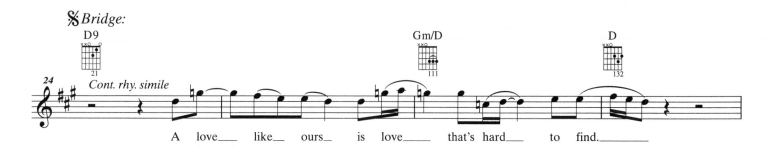

A love__ like__ ours__ is love____ that's hard__ to find._____

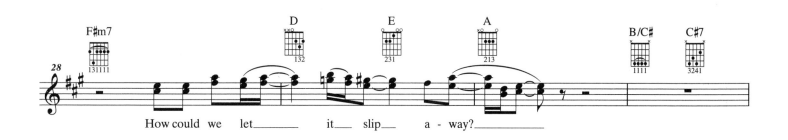

How could we let_____ it__ slip__ a - way?_____

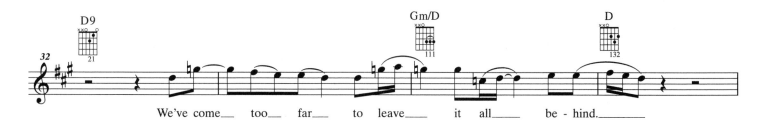

We've come__ too__ far__ to leave____ it all____ be - hind._____

If You Leave Me Now - 4 - 3

I DON'T WANT TO MISS A THING

(from *Armageddon*)

Words and Music by
DIANE WARREN

*Chord frames are suggested.

KISS FROM A ROSE

Words and Music by
SEAL

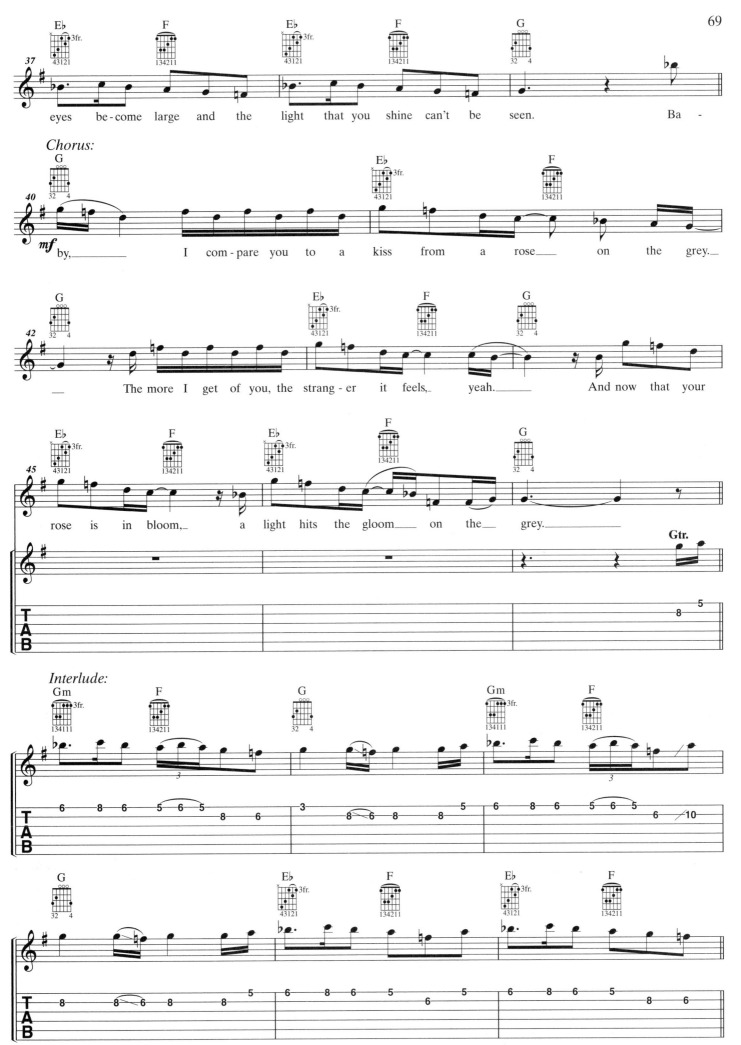

Kiss from a Rose - 5 - 3

70

Kiss from a Rose - 5 - 4

Kiss from a Rose - 5 - 5

KNOCKIN' ON HEAVEN'S DOOR

Words and Music by
BOB DYLAN

1. Ma - ma, take this___ badge off___ of me,
2. Ma - ma, put my___ guns in___ the ground,

I can't use___ it an - y - more.
I can't shoot___ them an - y - more.

Knockin' on Heaven's Door - 2 - 1

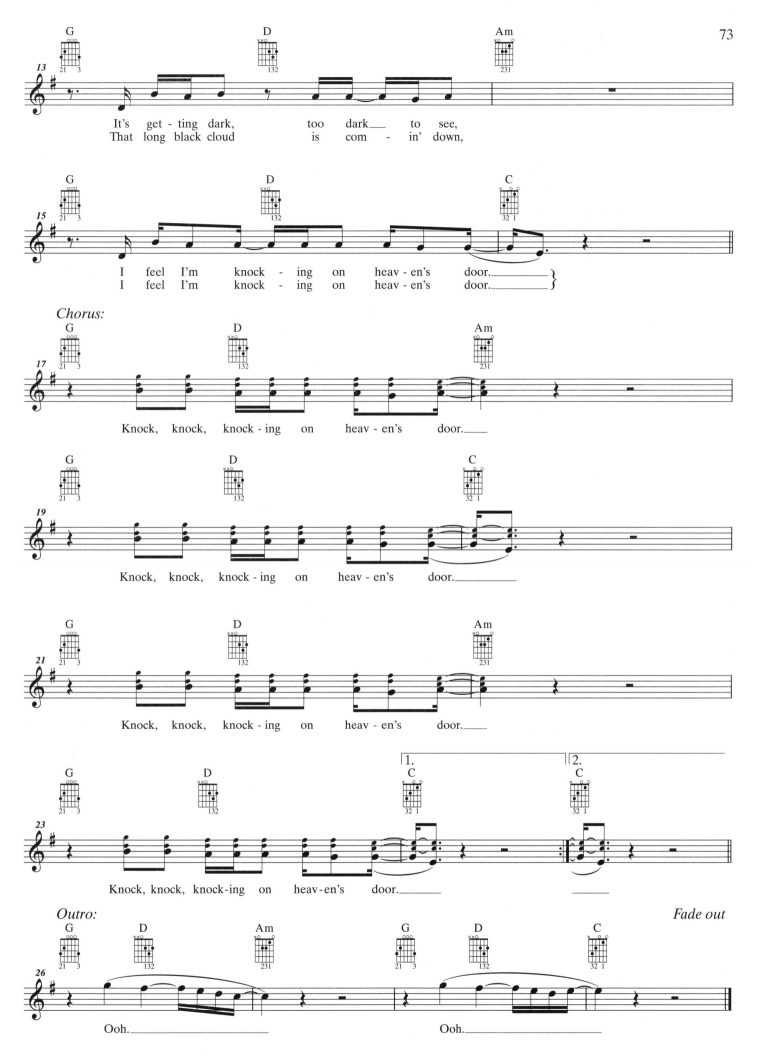

THE LOAD-OUT

Words and Music by
JACKSON BROWNE and BRYAN GAROFALO

The Load-Out - 9 - 1

Verse 1:

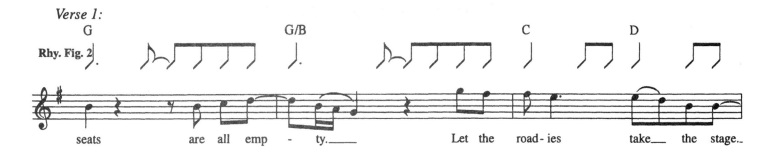

seats   are all emp - ty.___   Let the road - ies   take___ the stage..

___   Pack it up and   tear it down.___   They're the

first to come   and the last to leave,___ work - ing for that___ min - i - mum wage.

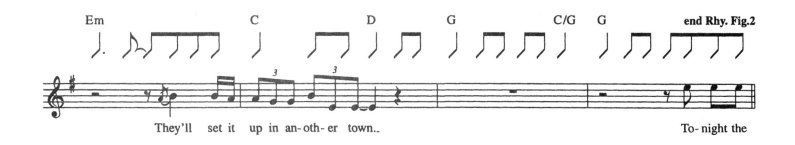

They'll set it up in an - oth - er town..   To - night the

peo - ple___ were so___ fine.   They wait - ed there in line.___   And when they

The Load-Out - 9 - 2

Keyboard Solo:
w/Rhy. Fig. 1 *(Gtr. 1) simile*

MY IMMORTAL

Words and Music by
BEN MOODY, AMY LEE and DAVID HODGES

To match recording, capo at 2nd fret.

Slowly and freely ♩ = 80

My Immortal - 3 - 1

Verse 2:
You used to captivate me
By your resonating light.
But, now I'm bound by the life you left behind.
Your face, it haunts
My once pleasant dreams.
Your voice, it chased away
All the sanity in me.
These wounds won't seem to heal.
This pain is just too real.
There's just too much that time can not erase.
(To Chorus:)

MARRY ME

Words and Music by
SAM HOLLANDER and PAT MONAHAN

1. For-ev-er could nev-er be long e-nough__ for me   to
2. To-geth-er can nev-er be close e-nough__ for me   to

Marry Me - 4 - 1

NIGHTS IN WHITE SATIN

Words and Music by
JUSTIN HAYWARD

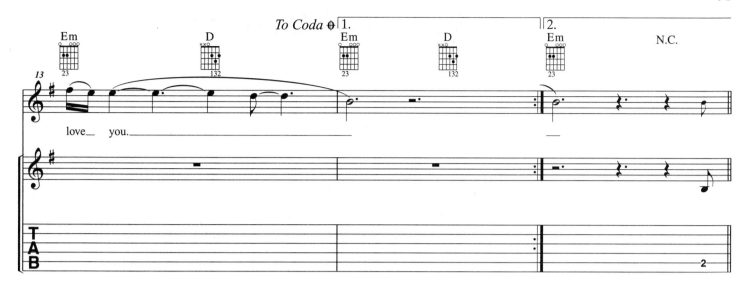

love__ you._____

Interlude:

Acous. Gtr. cont. strumming simile

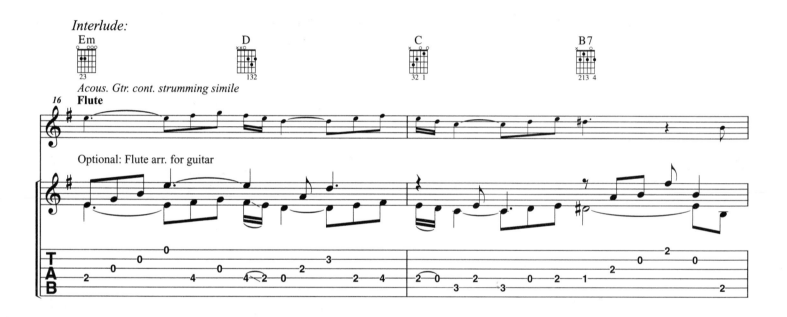

Optional: Flute arr. for guitar

Nights in White Satin - 4 - 2

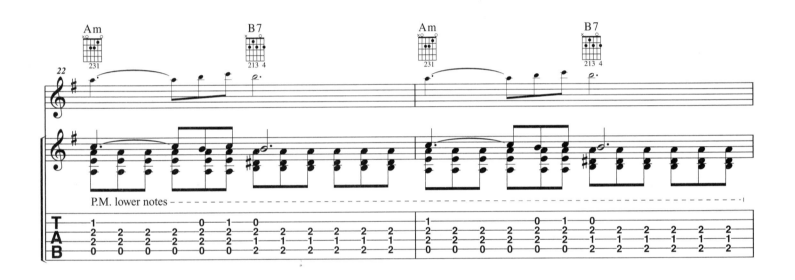

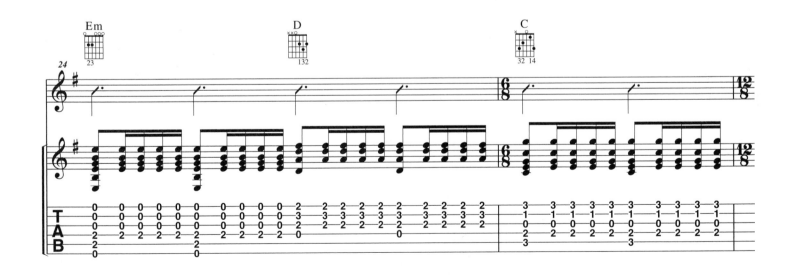

D.S. % al Coda

Verse 2:
Gazing at people.
Some hand in hand,
Just what I'm going through
They can't understand.
Some try to tell me
Thoughts they can not defend.
Just what you want to be
You'll be in the end.
And I love you,
Yes, I love you.
Oh, how I love you.
(To Interlude:)

ONE THING

All gtrs. in Drop D, down 1/2 step:

⑥ = D♭ ③ = G♭
⑤ = A♭ ② = B♭
④ = D♭ ① = E♭

Words and Music by
SCOTT ANDERSON and JAMES BLACK

Moderately slow ♩ = 76

Intro:

Play 4 times

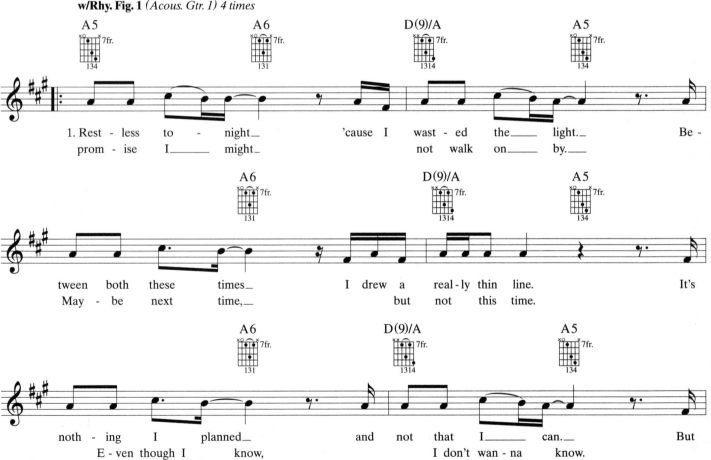

*Recording sounds a half step lower than written.

Verses 1 & 2:

w/Rhy. Fig. 1 *(Acous. Gtr. 1) 4 times*

1. Rest - less to - night__ 'cause I wast - ed the__ light.__ Be -
prom - ise I__ might__ not walk on__ by.__

tween both these times__ I drew a real - ly thin line. It's
May - be next time,__ but not this time.

noth - ing I planned__ and not that I__ can. But
E - ven though I know, I don't wan - na know.

One Thing - 4 - 1

One Thing - 4 - 2

ONLY THE LONELY

Words and Music by
MARTHA DAVIS

Chorus:

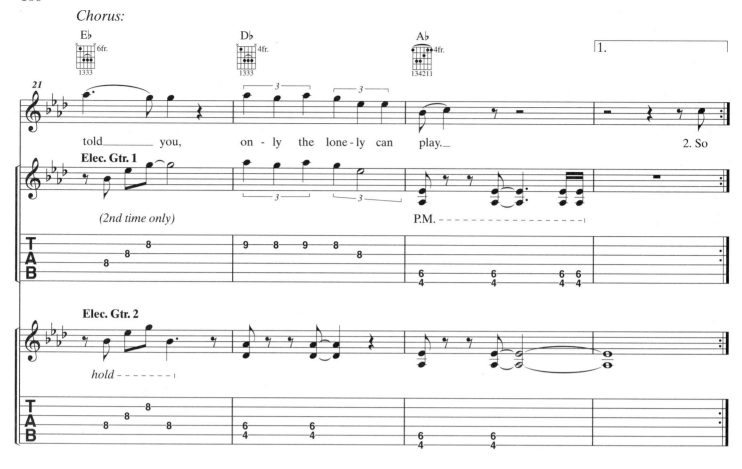

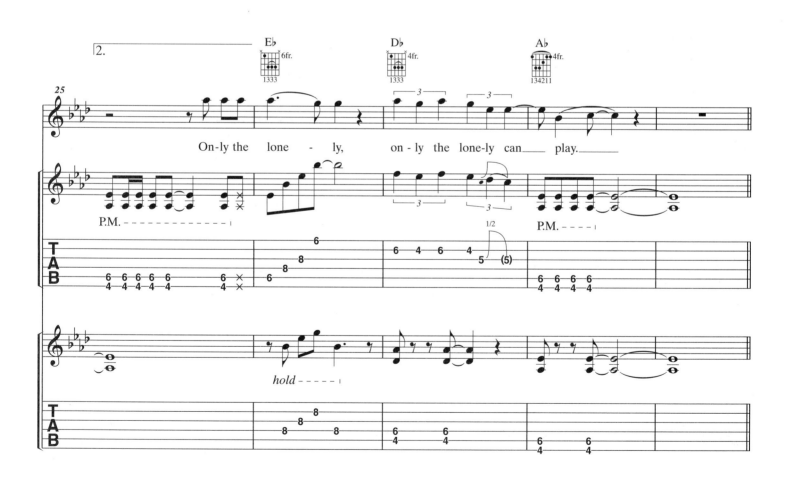

OPEN ARMS

Moderately slow ♩ = 104

Words and Music by
JONATHAN CAIN and STEVE PERRY

PATIENCE

To match recording, tune all gtrs. down 1/2 step:

⑥ = E♭   ③ = G♭
⑤ = A♭   ② = B♭
④ = D♭   ① = E♭

Words and Music by
W. AXL ROSE, SLASH, IZZY STRADLIN,
DUFF McKAGAN and STEVEN ADLER

Moderately ♩ = 120 w/half-time feel

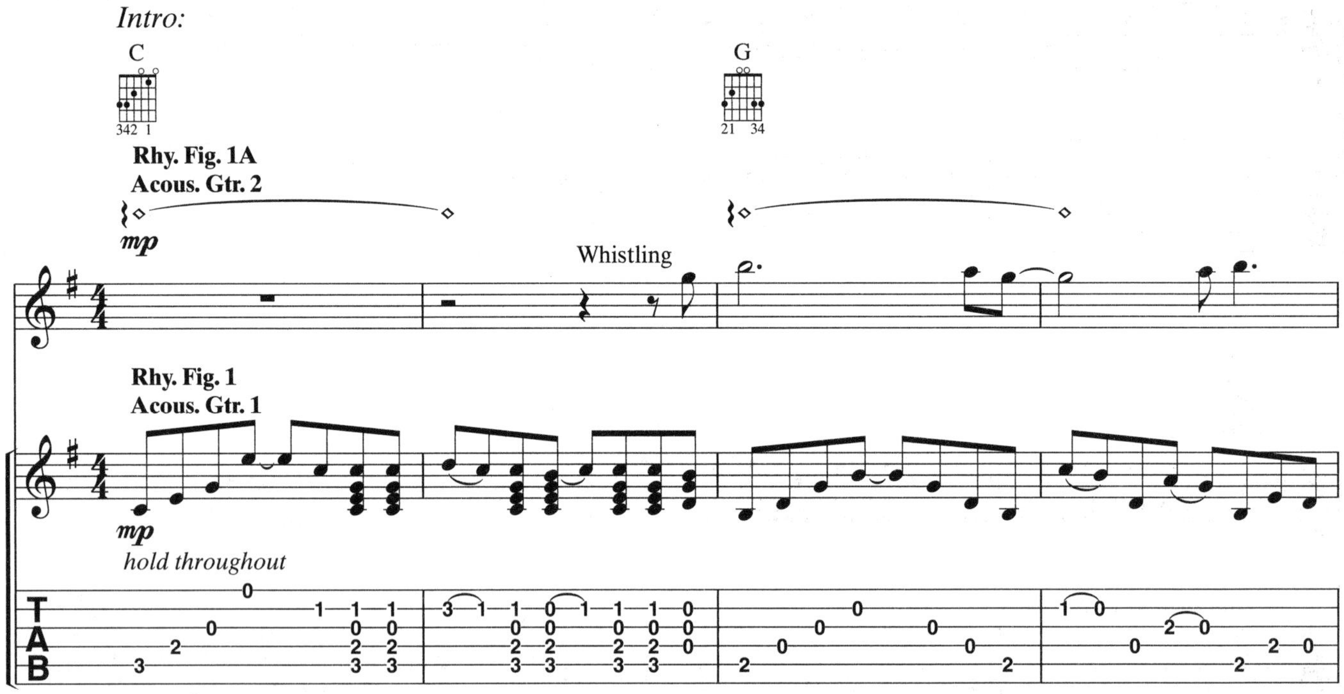

Verse:

Slow ♩ = 64

Outro:

STAIRWAY TO HEAVEN

Words and Music by
JIMMY PAGE and ROBERT PLANT

Verse 1:

There's a la - dy who's sure all that glit - ters is gold__ and she's buy - ing__ a stair - way to heav - en. When she gets there she knows,__ if the stores are all closed,__ with a word she__ can get what she came__ for.

Ooh,_____ ooo,_____ ooo,__ and she's buy - ing a stair - way__ to heav - en. There's a sign on the wall,__ but she wants to be sure,__ 'cause you

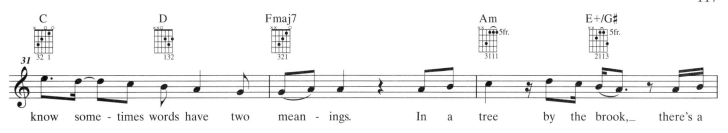

know some-times words have two mean-ings. In a tree by the brook,__ there's a

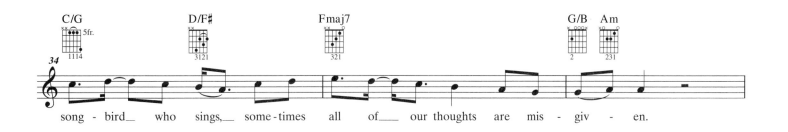

song-bird__ who sings,__ some-times all of__ our thoughts are mis-giv- en.

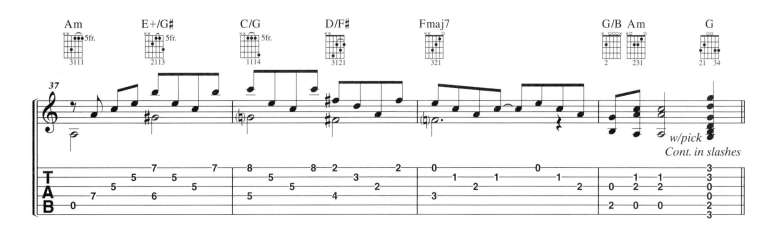

w/pick
Cont. in slashes

Interlude:

Rhy. Fig. 1

Ooh,_____ it makes we won - der.

end Rhy. Fig. 1

Ooh,_____ it makes me won - der._____ 2. There's a

118

120

Stairway to Heaven - 9 - 6

122 *Bridge:* ♩ = **102**

Stairway to Heaven - 9 - 8

to be a rock___ and not to roll.___

And she's buy - ing a stair - way___ to heav - en.___

Stairway to Heaven - 9 - 9

THANK YOU

Slowly ♩ = 78

Intro:
Fade in

Words and Music by
JIMMY PAGE and ROBERT PLANT

Verse 1:
Acous. Gtr. tacet

*Elec. Gtr. tacet

If the sun re-fused___ to shine,   I would still be
*Chords implied by organ.

Guitar Solo:

Elec. Gtr. cont. interlude fig. simile

Acous. Gtr.

Verse 2:

*Acous. & Elec. Gtrs. tacet

Elec. Gtr.

And so to - day__ my world,__ it smiles,____ your hand in mine,_

Acous. Gtr.

Thank You - 6 - 4

*Chords implied by organ.

*Part "echoed" one beat later by Acous. Gtr.

*Chords implied by organ.

WHEN I SEE YOU SMILE

Words and Music by
DIANE WARREN

Moderately fast (with a half-time feel) ♩ = 136

Intro:

Keybd.

mp

Verse 1:

Gtr.
mp

Cont. rhy. simile

Some-times I won-der if I'd ev-er make it through,_ through this world_ with-out

hav-ing you._ I just would-n't have a clue._

Verses 2 & 3:

Cont. verse rhy. simile

2. 'Cause some-times it seems like this world's clos-in' in on me_ and there's no way of
3. Ba-by, there's noth-in' in this world that could ev-er do what the touch of_ your

break-in' free_ and then I see you reach for me._
hand can do,_ it's like noth-in' that I ev-er knew._

Pre-chorus:

Some-times_ I wan-na give up wan-na give in. I wan-na quit the fight._
And when_ the rain is fall-ing I don't feel it, 'cause you're here with me._

When I See You Smile - 4 - 1

Pre-chorus:

Some - times__ I wan - na give up, I wan - na give in, I wan - na

quit the fight. Then one look at you, ba - by, and

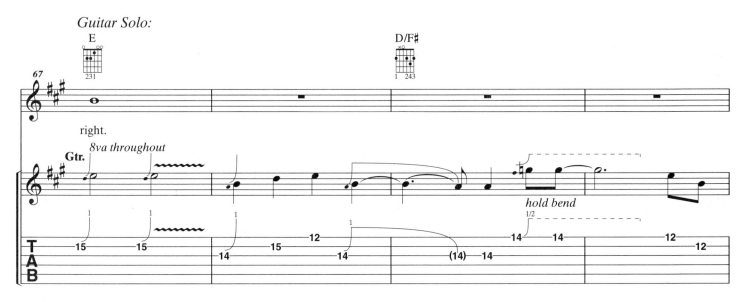

ev - 'ry - thing's__ al-right, ev - 'ry - thing's__ al-right. It's al -

Guitar Solo:

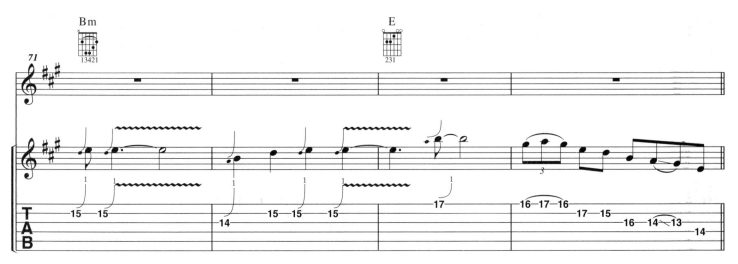

right.

Chorus:

A WHITER SHADE OF PALE

Words and Music by
KEITH REID and GARY BROOKER

1. We skipped the light fan - dan - go,_____ turned cart - wheels_ 'cross the
2. *See additional lyrics*

floor._ I was feel - ing_____ kind - a sea - sick,_

the crowd called out_____ for more._____ The room was hum - ming hard-

- er, as the ceil - ing flew a - way._

When we called out for an - oth - er drink,_____ the wait - er brought_ a tray._

A Whiter Shade of Pale - 2 - 1

Verse 2:
She said, "There is no reason
And the truth is plain to see."
But I wandered through my playing cards,
And would not let her be
One of sixteen vestal virgins
who were leaving for the coast.
And, although my eyes were open,
They might have just as well've been closed.
And so it was that later,
As the miller told his tale,
That her face, at first just ghostly,
Turned a whiter shade of pale.

A Whiter Shade of Pale - 2 - 2

WILD HORSES

Words and Music by
MICK JAGGER and **KEITH RICHARDS**

Moderately slow ♩ = 71

*Acous. Gtr. is a composite of 6-string and 12-string acous. gtrs.

1. Child - hood liv - ing___ is eas - y to do.___
2. I watched you suf - fer___ a dull___ ach - ing pain.___
3. I know I dreamed_ you___ a sin___ and a lie.___

*Elec. Gtr. simile on repeats.

WITH ARMS WIDE OPEN

Gtr. tuned in Drop D:
⑥ = D   ③ = G
⑤ = A   ② = B
④ = D   ① = E

Words and Music by
MARK TREMONTI and SCOTT STAPP

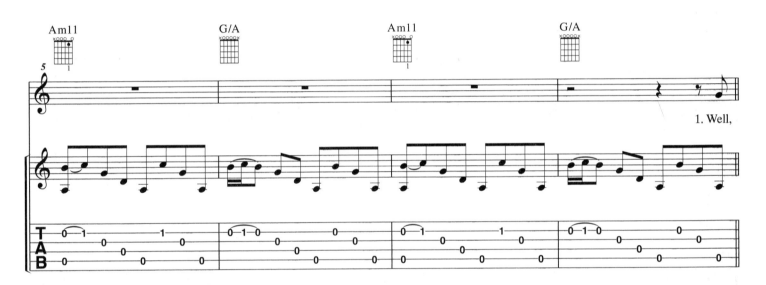

Verse:

With Arms Wide Open - 5 - 1

144

With Arms Wide Open - 5 - 5